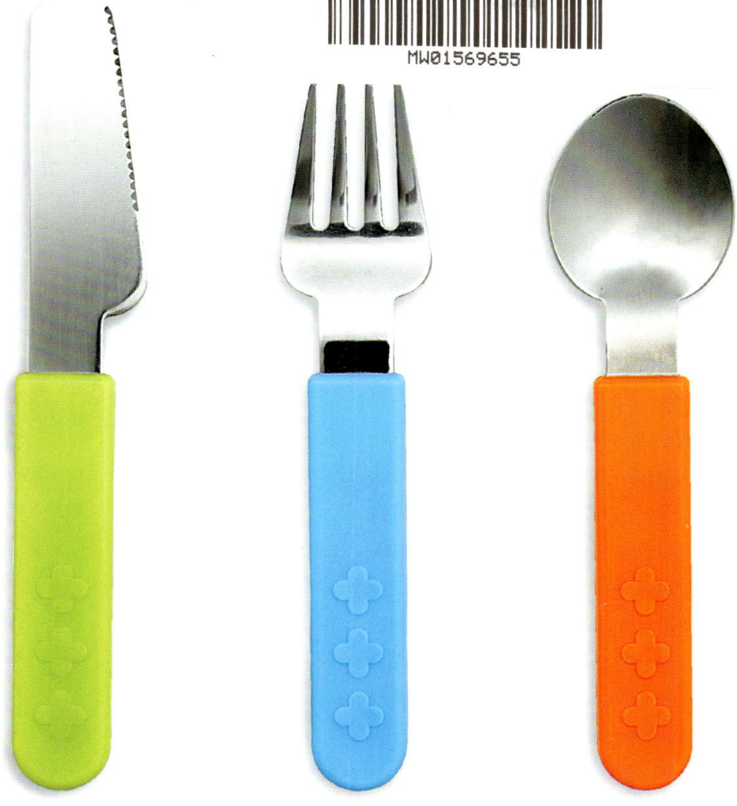

knife fork spoon

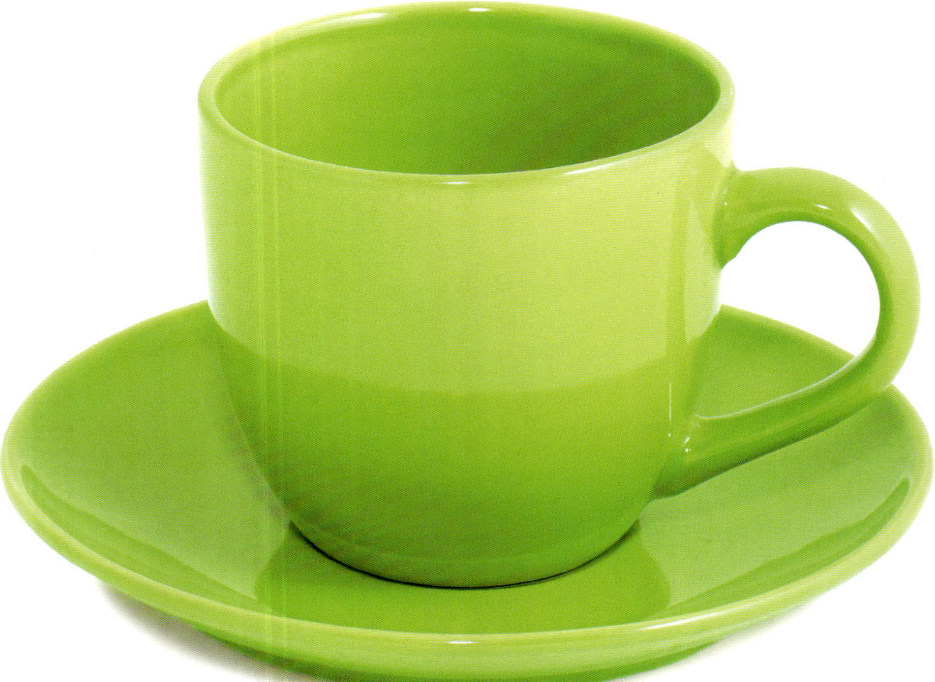

cup

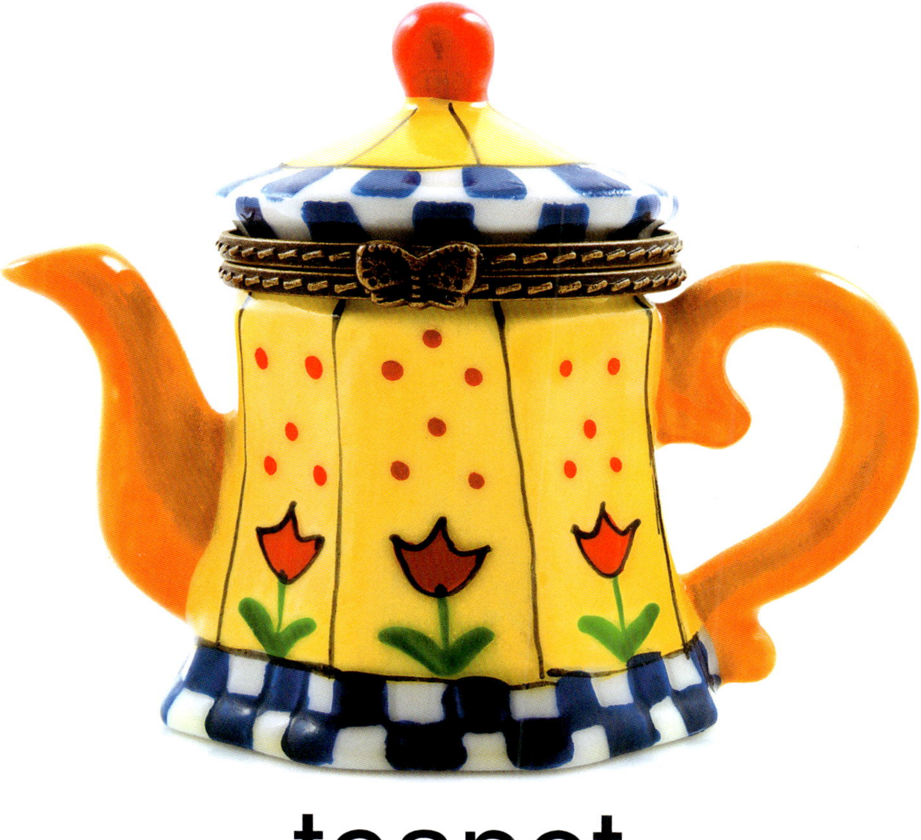

teapot

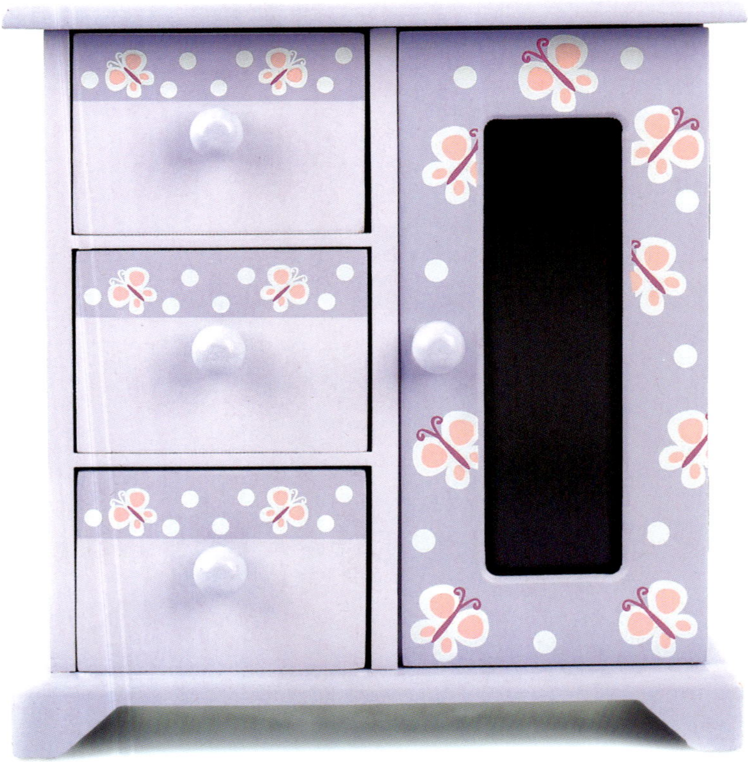

wardrobe

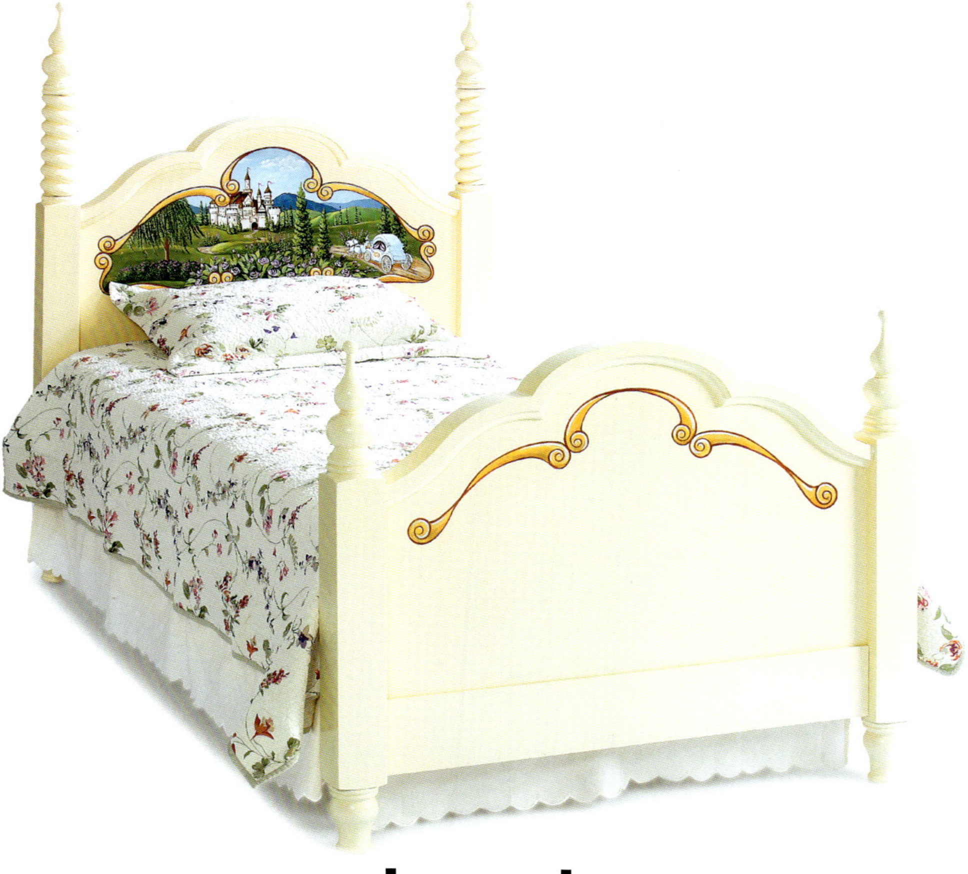

bed

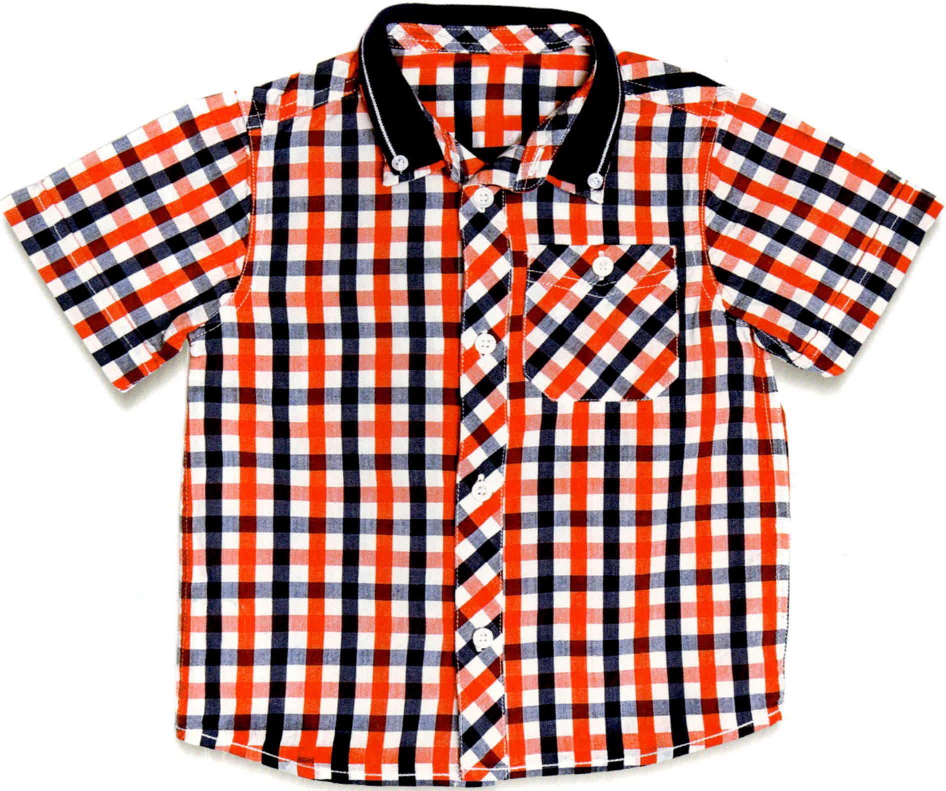

shirt

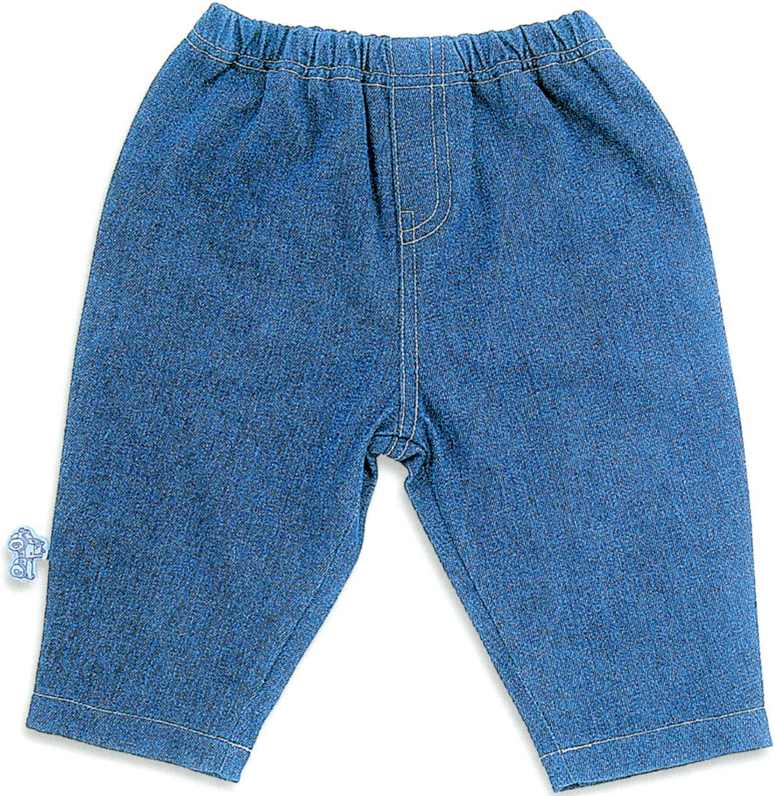

pants

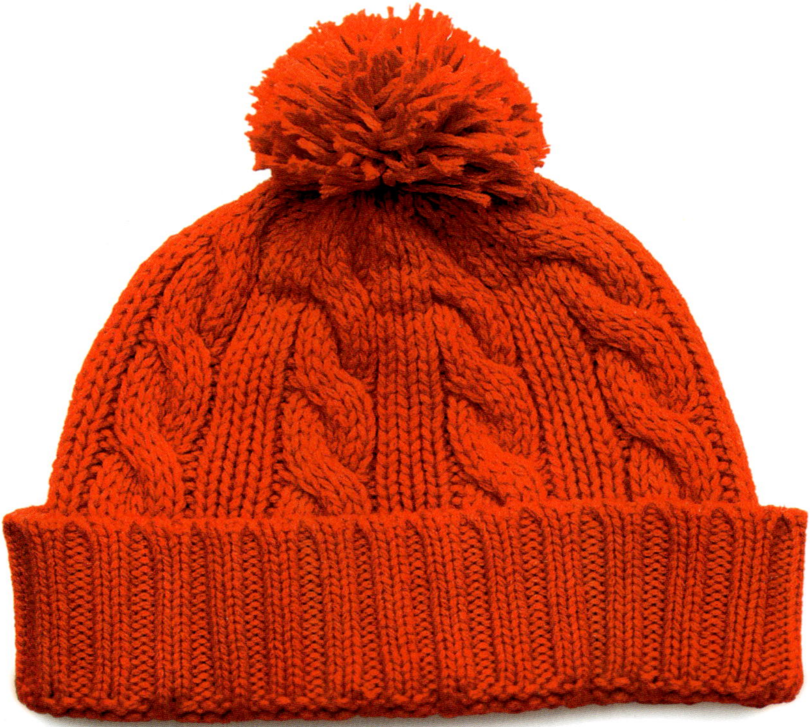

hat

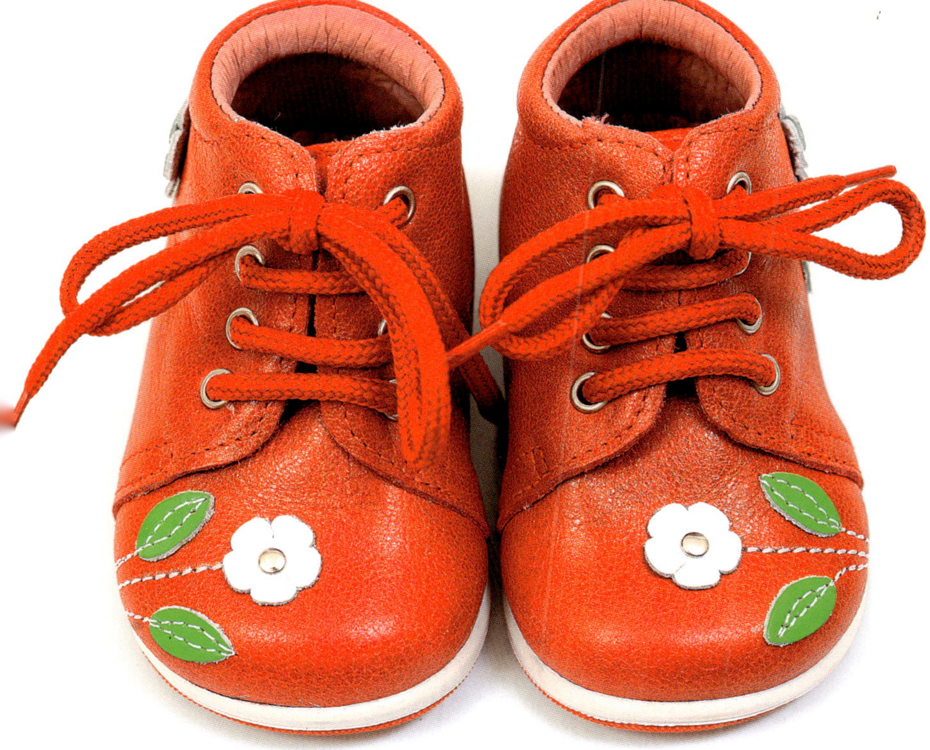

shoes

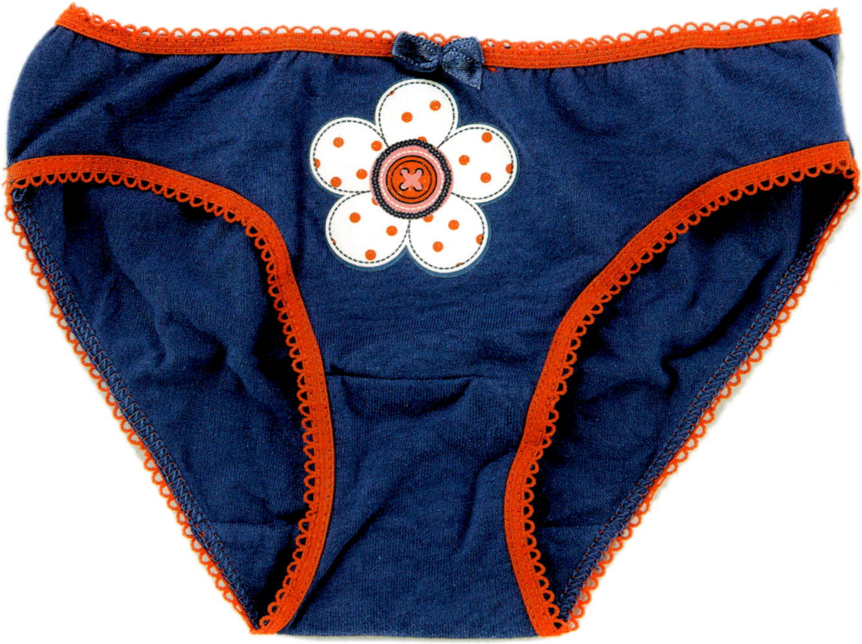

underwear

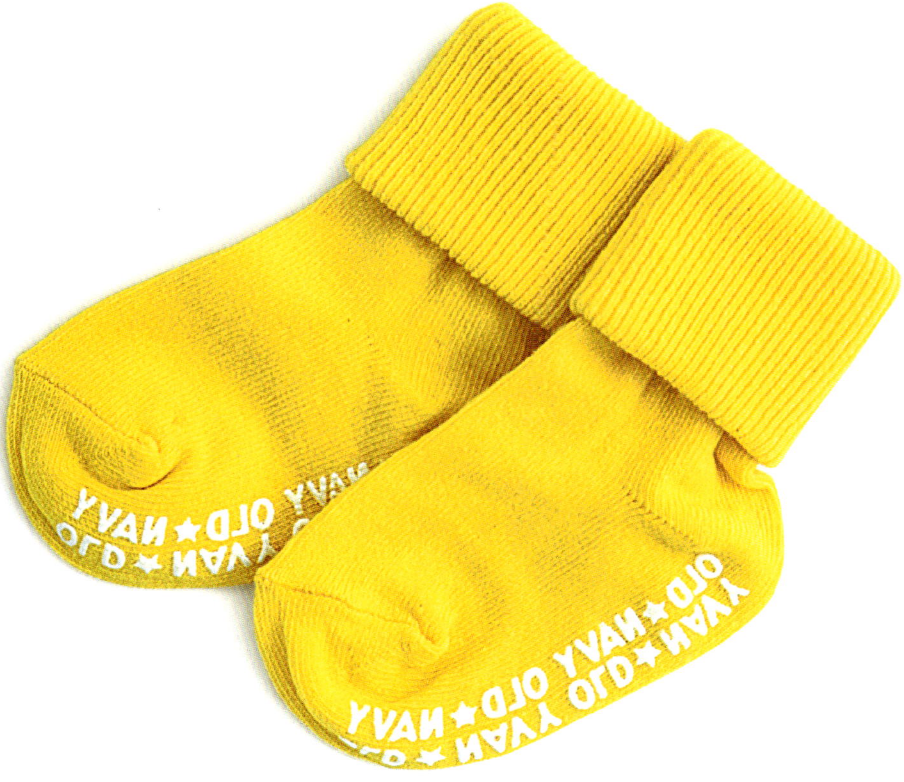

socks

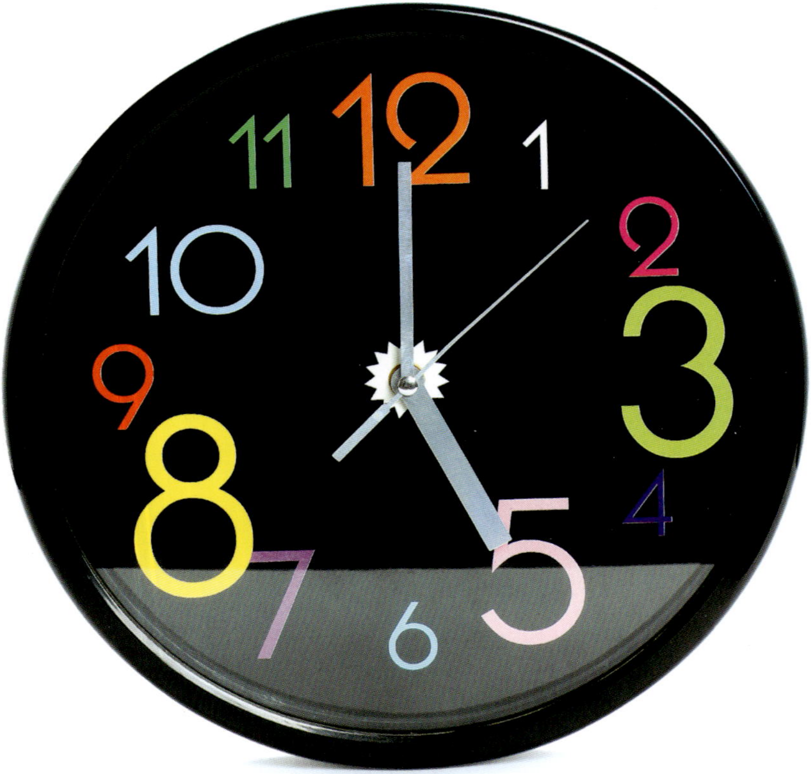

clock